A CHRISTIAN RESPONSE TO DUNGEONS AND DRAGONS

Other books by Peter Leithart:

The Reduction of Christianity, 1987 [with Gary DeMar]

Other books by George Grant:

Bringing in the Sheaves: Transforming Poverty into Productivity, 1985

In the Shadow of Plenty: Biblical Principles of Welfare and Poverty, 1986

The Dispossessed: Homelessness in America, 1986

The Changing of the Guard: Biblical Principles of Political Action, 1987

Rebuilding the Walls: A Biblical Strategy to Restore America's Greatness, 1987 [with Peter Waldron]

The Big Lie: The Scandal of Planned Parenthood, 1988

A CHRISTIAN RESPONSE TO DUNGEONS AND DRAGONS

The Catechism of the New Age

Peter Leithart
and
George Grant

Dominion Press
Fort Worth, Texas

Dedicated to our children:
May they ever be able to discern the difference.
Philippians 1:9-11

Special thanks to Jim Stewart and Robert Saxon, former Dungeon Masters, for their evaluation and input on this project.

Published by Dominion Press
7112 Burns Street
Fort Worth, Texas 76118

Printed in the U.S.A.

Library of Congress Catalog Card Number 87-071865
ISBN 0-930462-60-2

A CHRISTIAN RESPONSE TO
DUNGEONS AND DRAGONS
The Catechism of the New Age

Parents are concerned.

And well we should be. Our children are growing up in a very hazardous world. Not only are they forced to pick their way through a complex maze of conflicting values at school, in the neighborhood, and out in the marketplace, but they are even being assaulted in the "safety" of their own homes.

Across the airwaves has come a barrage of violent, irreverent, fantastic, and occultic Saturday morning cartoons. Out of the toy box has come a haunting phalanx of magical and monstrous macho images! Off the bookshelf has come a frightening parade of pulp and pap: comics and paperback books that exalt the basest of vices and disdain the highest of virtues. And then, of course, there is MTV: sex, drugs, violence, rebellion, and defilement on tap twenty-four hours a day, all at the flick of a switch and the turn of a dial.

The seductive siren's song of the world has begun to seep into even the most protected of environments. And as a result, the hearts and minds and souls of our children have become a battleground.

Amazingly though, the chief weapon used in this spiritual raid on our children is a game — just a simple little game. It is called *Dungeons and Dragons*. Even more than all the cartoons, toys, comics, books, videos, and music, this simple little game has served to make our children a "generation at risk."

What is Dungeons and Dragons?

It's Christmas morning. Brimming with excitement Junior opens his first gift, a *Basic Dungeons and Dragons Set*. Inside he finds a rule book, some graph paper, and an odd set of dice. No game board. No little "men" to move around. He checks the wrapping paper for miss-

1

ing pieces, then begins to open the other packages, hoping to find "the rest" of his game.

But, Junior has all he needs to play *Dungeons and Dragons* (*D&D*), the granddaddy of the fantasy role playing games (FRPs) and one of the fastest selling games in the United States. The game, you see, doesn't take place on a board. Instead, you play in your head. In *D&D* the basic rule is, "Use your imagination. Stretch it to the limit." Game boards and little men can be *so* confining.

There are rules, of course. Thousands and thousands of them. But the whole point of an FRP is to play a character whose actions are dictated by your imagination, not by the rules. Like drama without a script, *D&D* is so complicated that we can give only the barest description of how the game is played. Before the game begins, each player must define his character. A roll of the dice determines the character's basic personality. Seven areas are rated: strength, intelligence, wisdom, dexterity, constitution, comeliness and charisma. Another roll of the dice decides each character's age, diseases, parasitic infestations, and special skills.

Next, the player selects his character's race and class. If he wants to be a non-human, there are several races to choose from: dwarf, elf, gnome, half-elf, halfling, half-orc. Each race, in turn, is divided into several classes such as clerics, fighters, magic-users, and thieves. A player chooses his character's class according to the character's strengths. A character with high strength rating and low intelligence might be a Fighter. An intelligent character would be a good Magic-User or Cleric.

Then, the player rolls the dice to determine "hit points," the damage his character can suffer without dying. The higher the roll, the better his chance of surviving a melee.

Each character is given a certain amount of gold to buy equipment for his adventure. Different sorts of characters use different equipment. A Cleric purchases holy water, a Fighter needs heavy weapons, a Thief can obtain a prepackaged set of thievery tools.

Finally, the players choose their character's "alignment" from three basic possibilities: Law, Chaos, and Neutral. Lawful characters value order, organization, and the group, while those aligned with chaos value freedom, spontaneity, and the individual. Each alignment includes good and evil characters. The good characters operate in terms of "creature rights," while evil characters have no regard for their fellows. A character's alignment might be chaotic good, chaotic evil, lawful good, lawful evil, neutral evil, etc.

The Dungeon Master (DM) is the most important "player," though he doesn't really play the game at all. The DM is an experienced player who draws up the "game board," a complex dungeon map that is different in every game. He populates the dungeon with monsters selected from the rule book. Only the DM sees the map at the beginning of the game. He directs the players through the maze, telling them when they meet a monster, what kind of monster it is, and their chances of killing it. The outcome of a battle is determined by a dice roll. The players draw maps as they go. They enter the dungeon and battle the monsters, seeking treasure and trying to survive.

Unlike conventional games, there is no real end to *D&D*. A typical session can last 4-12 hours. Games can continue for years if the players are skillful enough to survive battles. As they conquer various monsters, in fact, they gain experience points and become more powerful and better equipped for battle. There aren't winners and losers in any conventional sense; only a series of adventures that finally come to an end when a character dies.

The Genesis of the Game

Dungeons and Dragons was invented by Gary Gygax, an enthusiast of historical war games that gained a cult following in the '50s and '60s. Gygax combined the war game idea with medieval imagery and magic to make *D&D*. Spurned by the major game companies, Gygax invested $1000 to form TSR Hobbies in 1973 to market his new creation. Brian Blume invested $2000 more in 1974, and the two began printing rule books.

At first sales were slow; the first 1000 games took a year to sell. The game gained in popularity during the following year, especially among college students. In 1975 TSR was incorporated, and Gygax and Blume began working fulltime. They published revised and advanced rule books and began to produce other FRPs. By 1977 sales were up to $564,000 and nearly a dozen employees had been added to the payroll.

It was not until 1979 that *D&D* gained nationwide attention. In that year, Michigan State University student James Dallas Egbert, a 16-year-old mathematics genius, disappeared, apparently while playing a realistic form of *D&D*, in the maze of steam tunnels underneath the University's campus. Egbert was found, but committed suicide a year later. His disappearance, and his obsession with *D&D* along with it, became front-page news in many major periodicals. Though most media assessments of the game were negative, the publicity paid huge dividends. Dana Lombardy, a columnist for *Model Retailer*, says that TSR "should raise a foundation to this Egbert kid. Except for the disappearance of that boy and the resulting national exposure, TSR could have remained a steadily growing hobby-game company instead of a sky-rocketing one." Gygax agrees: "Ultimately, it was immeasurably helpful to us in name recognition. We ran out of stock!"

The numbers confirm this assessment. Sales exploded from $2.3 million in 1979 to $8.7 million in 1980. Since 1980, sales have nearly doubled every year: 1981 sales were $14 million; 1982 exceeded $22 million. By 1985 TSR was racking in more than $100 million in sales! As the company grew, it began hitting a new market. Originally, the primary market was college students. By 1980, 46 percent of the sales were to the 10-14 age group, and another 26 percent to ages 15-17. The game continues to be popular, however, among older students, even at Christian colleges and seminaries.

Meanwhile, TSR also diversified in several directions. An electronic version is now available, and *D&D* is coming out in French and German editions. New FRPs were created, with names like *Warlocks and Warriors*, *Knights of Camelot*, *Top Secret*, *Boot Hill*, and *Gamma World*. TSR publishes a monthly magazine, *The Dragon*, and the *Endless Quest* book series, the first four of which ranked in the top five among juvenile best sellers. A movie, *Dungeonmaster*, appeared a few years back. And a number of Saturday morning cartoons have been developed for both network and cable broadcasting.

While TSR is by far the largest company producing FRPs, accounting for nearly half the total industry sales, they are not without (often fierce) competition. There are about 400 FRPs now on the market. Most games continue the "medieval sorcery" motif that dominates *D&D*. The competitors include *Tunnels and Trolls*, *Chivalry and Sorcery*, *RuneQuest*, and *Arduin Grimoire*. In all, it has been estimated that 250,000-300,000 FRPs have been sold.

The motifs of FRPs are reinforced by all the other aspects of youth culture. Saturday morning cartoons feature the *Masters of the Universe*, muscle-bound barbarians living in a world of magicians, witches, and sorcerers. You can get *Masters of the Universe* dolls, balls, comic books, and videos. There's even a feminist version: *She-Ra, Princess of Power*. And then there are the *Smurfs* and the *Care Bears*: cute and cuddly but born out of the same mentality.

Since 1980, *D&D* and its imitators have entered the mainstream of American life. Public schools use *D&D* to teach reading and math skills. Highly intelligent students are particularly attracted by the complexity and excitement, and *D&D* is often used in classes of "gifted children." In Herber City, Utah, parental objections to *D&D* in the public school pressured the school board to discontinue its use. A Boy Scout post in Chattanooga uses *D&D*, and the game has been advertised in *Boys Life*, the official Scout magazine. Some Catholic schools are using *D&D*. Public libraries open their doors for training and game sessions.

The Moral Dilemma

So, why all the fuss? *D&D* sounds like a challenging and exciting new way to spend an evening. It must be educational; otherwise they wouldn't use it in public schools, right? Even the Boy Scouts use it. In the face of all this support, it seems almost un-American to suggest there are serious deficiencies with the game.

But there are serious defects. Very serious. In spite of the favorable financial results of the Egbert case, the eerie course of events cast a shadow over the entire industry. Remember the "Freeway Killer" Vernon Butts, who committed suicide in his jail cell in 1981 while being held as a suspect in a string of murders? Butts was an avid *D&D* player, who often communicated with visitors using a code developed as a part of his *D&D* involvement. Another isolated incident? Not hardly. Police reports around the country have connected FRP activity to more than a hundred suicide and murder cases.

Of course, not everyone who plays the game becomes suicidal or homicidal. Still, there are an awful lot of unsettling things going on here. One of the chief defenses of FRPs is that they stimulate the imagination. This is undeniably true. The question is whether we want our imagination (or that of our children) stimulated in this particular way. Consider, for example, the level of violence and crime in a typical *D&D* game. One psychologist wrote, "There is hardly a game in which the players do not indulge in murder, arson, torture, rape, or highway robbery." And he *likes* the game! The *Dungeon Master's Guide* lists Hitler among those historical characters who exhibited true *D&D* charisma.

It gets worse, because the violence in *D&D* is generally less graphic than in some of its imitators. Consider these characters from *The Monster Manual*:

Harpy: The Harpys attack, torture, and devour their charmed prey. What they do not want they foul with excrement.

Lizard Man: They are omnivorous, but lizard men are likely to prefer human flesh to other foods. In this regard they have been known to ambush humans, gather up the corpses and survivors as captives, and take the lot back to their lair for a rude and horrid feast.

Or, consider this selection from the "Critical Hit Table" of the rule book for *Arduin Grimoire*:

- Dice roll: 37-38; hit location: crotch/chest; results: genitals/breast torn off; shock.
- Dice roll:95; hit location: guts ripped out; results: 20 percent chance of tangling feet, die in 1-10 minutes.
- Dice roll: 100; hit location: head; results: head pulped and splattered over a wide area.

As one 18-year-old player put it, these are games "where you get to kill people and get away with it."

Much of the violence is sexually oriented. The cover of the *Eldrich Wizardry* supplement to the *D&D* rule book pictures a nude woman lying across a sacrificial altar, an image with both sexual and occultic overtones. Sado-masochism is listed among the insanities that a character might suffer. Non-violent sexual references also abound. Male characters often attempt to seduce female characters. One of the "minor malevolent effects" is satyriasis, defined as "excessive or abnormal sexual craving in the male." Herbal remedies for venereal diseases are provided in the rule book.

Those who profit from the games are quick to defend the emphasis on sex, violence, and sexual violence. Dave Hargrave, creator of *Arduin Grimoire*, says of his game:

It's deliberately gruesome. You have to blow a hole through that video shell the kids are encased in. They are little zombies. They don't know what pain is. They have never seen a friend taken out in a body bag. They've got to understand that what they do has consequences. The world is sex. The world is violence. It's going to destroy most of these kids when they leave TV-land.

An article in *The Dragon* made the same defense of *D&D* ethics:

Being evil and tough seems to have a lot of machismo and can draw quite a bit of respect for you in the game. . . .

Besides, what we're doing is the way of the universe. Only the strong survive. Nice guys finish last. I'm number one. Might makes right.

Quite explicably, the name of the game is power. Of all the characters, the Dungeon Master is clearly the most powerful. *D&D* enthusiasts have no hesitation in saying that the Dungeon Master is "God." But the other characters are equally motivated by lust for power. Power can be exercised by brute force or through magical spells. For some players, this motivation is transferred to real-life relationships. One young player admits that playing *D&D* encouraged him to be deceptive and manipulative at home and in school. He would purposely get into trouble just for the sake of testing his survival skills in a real-life crisis. He was especially attracted to Merlin, the magician of King Arthur's court.

> I thought it would be great to have Merlin's spirit inside of me; then I could do what he used to do. I tried to get deeper and deeper by playing *D&D*, playing the Ouija Board, reading horoscopes and even having my palm read. I really got into it a lot, and I would think inside of me that I wasn't scared of anything — I had power, too. I believed that I was too tough to be hurt — nothing could hurt me. I did things like jumping on a Doberman Pinscher that was chasing me and some guys, and walking off a ledge just to prove the power I had.

A frustrated writer admitted that he experienced "an incredible sense of power" as a Dungeon Master: "In some games, they don't call me Dungeon Master; they call me God."

Fantasy power is a strong attraction to many people who feel powerless in the real world. For such people, *D&D* becomes an escape from a drab and burdensome life. Advertisements for *D&D* play on this aspect: "I don't have to just hang around. I can play *Dungeons and Dragons*." The degree of escape varies. Some can leave the game behind them when a session is over. For others, *D&D* replaces life. They talk about nothing but their dungeon experiences. What began as a game becomes a life-dominating obsession. Such was the case with "John," a 16-year-old living in Southern California:

> I am the Dungeon Master 98 percent of the time. I am the God of my world, the creator who manipulates the gods and humans. But my bossiness has extended itself into real life. I've exploited and abused people. People have hated me for it. . . . Ever since I was ten, I've wanted to drop out of this world. There are so many

flaws. A lot of things are unfair. When I am in my world, I control my own world order. I can picture it all. The groves and trees. The beauty. I can hear the wind. The world isn't like that. . . . It's hazardous. . . . The more time you spend in your fantasy world, the more you want to walk away from the burdensome decisions in life. . . . The more I play *D&D*, the more I want to get away from this world.

No doubt, *D&D* did not create John's disillusionment, but it provided an outlet for the full expression of his autonomy and rebellion. In a very dramatic way, *D&D* reinforced John's hatred for life as ordered and given by God.

Obsessive escapism of this sort is virtually equivalent to schizophrenia. One psychologist warned that adolescents may become emotionally and mentally disturbed by obsessive participation in FRPs. "The greatest danger I see is the escape from reality. These kids take their own unacceptable impulses and put them into fantasy. Schizophrenia is a thought disorder and *D&D* confuses the way people think. Thoughts not based on reality are dangerous." One enthusiastic player admitted that *D&D* had made him a virtual schizophrenic. He said he would probably cry if the character he has been directing for three years were to die.

To this point, *D&D* might appear to be only a more graphic form of earlier war games. But the method of warfare in *D&D* is entirely different. Magic, witchcraft, casting spells — these are the most desirable and powerful weapons in FRPs. In fact, it is the occultic element that makes FRPs what they are; without them, they would be grotesque but essentially run-of-the-mill war games. It is the occultic element that gives players of *D&D* and its imitators the sense of awesome power. It is the occultic element that leads to a manipulative attitude. And it is the occultic element that makes the game so very dangerous. Magic and witchcraft are found on nearly every page of an FRP rule book. The list of characters from which a player chooses includes magic users, druids, illusionists, and clerics. There are two major types of spells described: magical and clerical. The characters with magical powers are the most powerful players in the game; the other characters rely on physical strength and savagery. The *Dungeon Master's Guide* includes several pages of instruction on acquiring and casting spells. There are directions for chanting, the use of familiar spirits, speaking with the dead, uses of occultic symbols to protect the spell caster, and definitions of special spells used by shamans and witchdoctors. Spells are given for healing, exorcism, charming other characters, magical flight, fireballs, divination, and even restoring the dead.

Many of the spells, incantations, symbols, and protective measures are genuine occultic techniques. Several spells, for example, instruct the player to draw a protective circle when communicating with demons, a practice used by real witches. Spells often require human blood or flesh. The spell for a Cacodemon (Conjuration) suggests that "By tribute of fresh human blood and the promise of one or more human sacrifices, the summoner can bargain with the demon for willing service." Another spell, smacking of Biblical references, gives instructions for changing sticks into snakes and back again.

The Dungeon Master also has a wide variety of monsters and demons to populate his dungeon. Many of these are drawn from Satanism. One monster, the Mane, is described as a sub-demon who has gone to the "666 layers of the demonic abyss." The most evil of them "are confined in tiers of flames of Gehenna." Baalzebub is listed as an archdemon. There are hell hounds, able to "breathe out a scorching fire on an opponent up to a one inch distance." The Rakshasa is described as an "evil spirit encased in flesh" who enjoys a diet of human flesh and has the powers of ESP and illusion. At the very least, anyone familiar with FRP rule books is learning the terminology of witchcraft and Satanism. More likely, a seed is sown and he is almost imperceptibly drawn into the occult.

Of course, the creators of FRPs deny that they are promoting witchcraft. Most claim that they don't believe in the stuff anyway. And besides, they insist, the characters in the game are fighting *against* these demons. Even some Christians have defended the game because of its realistic depiction of evil. *But, remember that it's not just the monsters who have Satanic powers. The heroes, the "good guys" also use magic and witchcraft and learn genuine spells and occult techniques.* Regardless of the intentions of the creators of FRPs, Dr. Gary North's summary is still accurate:

> Without any doubt in my mind, after years of study in the history of occultism, after having researched a book on the topic, and after having consulted with scholars in the field of historical research, I can say with confidence: these games are the most effective, most magnificently packaged, most profitably marketed, most thoroughly researched introduction to the occult in man's recorded history. Period.

According to the dictionary, a *catechism* is "a program of instruction containing a summary of the principles or an introduction to the fundamentals of a subject." Through the ages Christians have used catechisms to teach the ABCs of the faith to their children. By repetition and recitation the catechisms enabled them to rehearse Biblical basics in a fun, easy-to-learn fashion.

In an ominously parallel way, *D&D* has become a modern-day catechism. The game contains a summary of the principles and an introduction to the fundamentals of the occult. By repetition and recitation, *D&D* enables children to rehearse occultic basics in a fun, easy-to-learn fashion. Thus, *D&D* really is a catechism of occultism.

Instead of raising up a generation nurtured and admonished by the things of God, we're systematically weaning our children on the occult.

The Christian Response

How should a Christian respond to such games? For several reasons, we think they should be simply off limits to Christians. *First,* virtually all FRPs present a general world-view that is antithetical to Christianity, pure and simple. The games treat magic, witchcraft, and Satan as pure fantasy, while the Bible views these as awful realities. An avid player begins to treat these realities as fairy tales. We must put it even more strongly than this. Not only are gods, devils, and demons treated as fantasy, Jesus Himself is included as one of the deities. Note carefully the logic here: "It's just a game. The monsters aren't real. The magical powers aren't real. The gods aren't real. Jesus is one of the gods." Christ is reduced to the level of fantastic monsters, halflings, dwarves, and elves. We can give this no less a label than blasphemy.

Second, most FRPs takes place in a thoroughly Manichaean universe where law and chaos are equally powerful and, in a strange sense, equally "good." Characters can choose to align themselves with law or chaos, and each of these alignments can be good, evil, or neutral. There are good and evil deities. The spells suggest the use of "holy/unholy water." In such a universe, magic can be either white or black, good or evil. And it doesn't much matter which. Obsessive players who become deeply attached to their characters are training themselves to view reality in the same way.

Third, Scripture expressly forbids tampering with magic and witchcraft, divination, human sacrifice, and many of the other common elements of most FRPs (cf. Ex. 22:18; Deut. 19:9-14; Lev. 18:21; 19:26; 31). Saul was severely rebuked for practicing witchcraft (1 Samuel 15; 28). Witchcraft and divination are attempts to gain wisdom, favor, and power apart from God's ordained means, and thus involve a thorough rejection of God's authority. Witchcraft is associated in the Scripture with rebellion, idolatry, and adultery.

In defending FRPs, many people have pointed out the obvious fact that most fairy tales (The Brothers Grimm, J.R.R. Tolkien, or C.S. Lewis for example) are full of witches, goblins, and sorcerers. But the heroes of these stories aren't the witches and sorcerers. Only the evil witch can change the prince into a frog. The prince himself uses entirely mortal means. Sorcery is always a temptation in fairy tales. As Lewis' and Tolkien's mentor, G.K. Chesterton, pointed out, the genius of fairy tales lies in the fact that the hero is a normal person in an abnormal world, an innocent among ravaging nether beasts. Make the hero abnormal and you destroy the tension and interest (not to mention the moral focus) of the entire narrative. There's all the difference in the world between Hansel and a dwarf cleric who casts spells. Both may meet a witch, but they react differently. The dwarf covets the witch's power; Hansel just wants a chance to shove her into the oven.

How Should We Then Play?

We know, we know. This whole thing is just another way that Christians have found to spoil everyone's fun. We can't sleep at night if we know someone is having a good time. Because this caricature of Christianity is so commonplace, it is necessary for us to present the outlines of a Biblical approach to play in general and role-playing in particular.

Leisure is one of the chief blessings of God's covenant mercy. God delivers His people that they may *rest*. This is a central theme of *Exodus*. The book begins with Israel in slavery. Moses appears before Pharaoh to demand that the Israelites be permitted to celebrate a festal sacrifice (5:3). Instead, Pharaoh charges the Israelites with laziness and increases their burden (5:6-9, 17-18). After the Exodus, Israel observes a weekly Sabbath (16:23). Thus, in the recitation of the law in Deuteronomy, the Sabbath is a reminder of Israel's slavery (Deut. 5:15). Israel cannot deny rest to aliens because to do so would be to imitate Pharaoh and, as it were, to turn back the clock on redemptive history. It is for this reason that the Sabbath takes on such central importance in later Israelite history. To neglect the Sabbath is to revert to a bondage where rest and leisure are denied. The Sabbath, of course, is centrally a religious rest and a time of worship. The point here is simply that leisure, "time out" from work, is an important and God-ordained part of the life of God's people.

By pushing this theme back to the beginning of Biblical history, we come to a fuller understanding of the nature of the Sabbath rest. While *Deuteronomy* roots the Sabbath in the Exodus, the book of *Exodus* (Ex. 20:4), roots it in creation: Israel is commanded to keep the Sabbath because the Lord Himself rested on the seventh day of creation week (Ex. 20.4). Thus, the leisure of God's people is to image the "leisure" of God. Significantly, God's rest follows His evaluation of creation as "very good" (Gen. 1:31). From this we can infer that God's seventh-day rest was not a mere cessation from labor, but a positive *enjoyment* of the "very good" things He had made. This is confirmed by *Proverbs* (Prov. 8:30-31), where God's Wisdom is pictured as a craftsman *delighting* in the world He has made, and especially in man (Prov. 8:30-31). Man's rest, in imitation of God, is to include this aspect of enjoyment of creation. Again, this is emphasized in *Genesis* (Gen. 2:9), where we are told that the trees were "pleasing to the eye and good for food (Gen. 2:9)." Man was made not only to rule creation, but also to enjoy God's bounty in it (Eccles. 2:24-26; 3:12-14; 5:18-20). Indeed, the Bible considers it a curse for a man to work without being able to enjoy the fruits of his labor (cf. Deut. 28:30; Is. 65:22). Freed from the crushing burden of guilt and sin, the believer is able fully to *enjoy* God's world.

Partying, laughter, and play are also included in the Biblical understanding of leisure. After the Exodus, Moses and Miriam led Israel in singing and dancing; David danced on the return of the ark to Jerusalem; Jeremiah compared Israel's return from exile to a virgin dancing and playing a tambourine and to a lavish banquet (Jer. 31:4, 10-14). These are all "religious" celebrations that nonetheless involve what older translations call "merrymaking." "Non-religious" play is also presented in Scripture as a blessing. The prophets, for example, predicted that in the Messianic age, children would *play* in the streets and at the nest of vipers (Zech. 8:5; Is. 11:7). The sight and sound of children safely playing in the streets is a sign of a well-ordered city.

But of course, our leisure must be subject to God's Law. Play is good, but the "play" of the Israelites at Sinai brought God's curse upon them (Ex. 32:6). Laughter is God's gift, but the laughter of Sarah arose from unbelief (Gen. 18:12ff). Parties are good, but the merriment of the rich man was foolish (Lk. 12:13-21). Moreover, leisure is never to *dominate* our lives; there is a time for everything under the sun. The modern idea that one works in order to have the wherewithal to play is not Biblical. The Preacher of *Ecclesiastes* says that we should enjoy our leisure *and* our work. He summarizes in this way: "Whatever your hand finds to do, do it with all your might" (Eccles. 9:10). Play, while good in itself, can never become an escape from responsibility.

What does the Bible say specifically about role-playing? Scripture seems to assume that role-playing, or imitation, is inescapable. We all imitate someone or something. Indeed, it is bound up in man's very being to be an imitator. We are first of all to imitate our Creator. But Scripture counsels us not only to imitate God, but to imitate those who are godly. Paul often tells his readers to imitate him (eg., 1 Cor. 4:16; 11:1; Phil. 3:17; etc.). The writer of *Hebrews* tells us to imitate the faithful men and women of the Old Testament, as well as the leaders of the Church (Heb. 6:12; 13:7). God even tells us to imitate animals. The lazy are counselled to imitate the ant (Pr. 6:6ff). And, we might suggest that the workaholic learn to imitate leviathan (Ps. 104:26).

This emphasis on imitation is confirmed by the Biblical under-standing of teaching and learning. Teaching and learning are not purely intellectual categories. When the Lord "taught warfare" to the Israelites (Judg. 3:2), He did not conduct a seminar in military strat-egy. He taught warfare by leaving foreign powers in the land for Israel to fight. Israel learned war by fighting. Teaching and learning in Scripture include intellectual and verbal instruction, but also include imitation or "role-playing," drill, practice, discipline, and the peda-gogy of ritual.

Thus, there seems to be every Scriptural reason for teaching through "role-playing" or "pretending." The value of this kind of training is seen most obviously in children. Our daughters learn something about motherhood by playing with their dolls. Our sons begin to learn courage by pretending to fight. This role-playing will pay dividends in later life. It's said that Abe Lincoln learned to speak by standing on a stump and delivering orations to a pile of split rails.

There is also room for non-didactic role-playing, that is, for role-playing "just for fun." The lovers in the *Song of Songs* appear to be engaging in playful role-playing. In the Feast of Tabernacles, the Israelites lived in "booths" for a week. The primary purpose was didactic, to remind Israel of their deliverance from slavery into the abundance of the land. But it is hard to resist the suspicion that the "role-play" also contributed to the *festive* atmosphere. In any case, a certain level of identification with a role is basic to playing games and enjoying fiction and drama.

There are, however, limits to our role-playing. The most obvious is that we are not to imitate those who are rebels against God. Role-play is a powerful means of teaching new behavior. To play the role of a rebel is to learn rebellion. Thus, the Lord commanded Israel not to imitate the nations (Deut. 18:9; lit., "You shall not learn to do according to the abominations of the nations"). This passage is especially significant for our purposes, because Israel is specifically forbidden to imitate the foreign nations in human sacrifice, witchcraft, and divination.

The second limitation on role-playing is that the role can never become an identification. This was Adam's sin. He was created to imitate God, but he wanted to *be* God. We are told to imitate the ant, but to become an ant is a Kafkaesque nightmare. It is always dangerous to become so attached to a role model that one cannot separate himself from that role. In some cases, the danger can be explicit, like the child who jumps out of a window thinking he's Superman. In other cases, the danger is more subtle; a confusion of identity can take place. Sometimes, the identification is relatively innocuous, such as when a player begins to take a game too seriously. Ultimately, all extreme identification with a role is sin, because it involves a rebellious rejection of the role to which God has assigned us. This motive is apparent in many of the *D&D* enthusiasts quoted above. They hate their God-given role in the God-directed drama of history, and they play *D&D* in order to create their own identity and their own history.

The issue, then, is not role-playing or no role-playing, but *which roles* and *how intensely involved* do we become. There is no good reason to play characters who regularly practice what God condemns. The power of role-play is such that we take on some of the character of the roles we play. Role-playing has sometimes been used as a brainwashing technique and is regularly used by psychologists and humanistic educators as a way to teach new behavior. These effects could be positive, if only the roles they thrust upon their subjects were positive. After all, some behavior *needs* to be changed, and role-play could be a helpful way to learn better habits. But if the roles involve the use of pop-psychology, New Age educational manipulation, witchcraft, deception, and gratuitous violence, the habits learned are bound to be bad ones.

The short of it is that *any* activity that is not submitted to the rule of God's Law is bound to turn ugly and dangerous. On the other hand, any activity that *is* submitted to the rule of God's Law is bound to strengthen and edify.

So, what do we say to children who play with toy guns and plastic soldiers? Is not this a role-playing activity that can lead to violent behavior? It certainly can, if the child takes his play role so seriously that he begins to bully children in, say, Sunday school class. But war is, Biblically speaking, a legitimate, though undesirable, use of violence. By learning to play war, a child is not necessarily learning to do anything that God forbids. Indeed, such play can be helpful to instill in a child the reality of the Christian's life-long warfare against Satan and sin.

Or what about playing evil characters in drama? May a Christian legitimately play Iago? Mephistopheles? Ted Bundy? Charles Manson? Clearly, the character's place in the entire context of the work is the decisive factor. If a play celebrates the perversion of its character, there can be little justification for a Christian playing the role. And, there is the factor of identification with the role. Lee J. Cobb was so intensely involved in his portrayal of Willy Loman that he began to contemplate suicide. This is clearly a sinful level of identification.

In summary, Scripture *encourages* leisure, play, and even role-playing, though always within the limits of the moral Law. In the context of these standards, however, our imaginations find true freedom. Like the sheep to which Scripture so often compares us, our freest play is within the fold. Outside, there is only the bondage of fear that allows for no real leisure.

Practical Matters

Okay. So now, what's a parent to do? How can we both protect our children from the evil effects of *Dungeons and Dragons* and teach them a healthy Biblical perspective of play?

First, as parents we must make certain that our families begin to build a spiritual life together. Simply going to Church on Sundays is not enough. A family needs to *pray* together, *study* the Bible together, and *celebrate* the seasons together. Our children need to see us modeling a fully orbed comprehensive Christian walk that touches every area of life. And they must be invited to walk that walk with us.

Second, as parents we must make certain that our families have plenty of fun together. By watching *us* have fun, our children learn how to have good, wholesome fun. By watching *our* friendships in action, they learn how to make godly friendships. By watching *us* play, they see what righteous recreation is like. And by including our children in our fun, our friendships, and our play, we beckon them to walk in our footsteps. That is the essence of discipleship. And that is the essence of parenting: teaching by doing.

Third, as parents we must *explain* our rules to our children. It is not enough to say "no." Our children need to know why we've said "no." If we don't want to let them watch some of the Saturday morning cartoons that "*all* the other kids" watch, then we ought to offer a reasonable and Scriptural explanation. Perhaps we can even turn the programs on for a few minutes every once in a while, pointing out the problems to our children and providing them with the basic tools they'll need to exercise discernment themselves. Don't just say "no" to *Dungeons and Dragons*, or anything else. We must equip our children so that *they* can say "no" without *us* having to say a thing.

Fourth, as parents we need to provide the *right* kind of entertainment for our families. Good books should always be available. And they should be read. Why not read a chapter of C. S. Lewis' Narnia series before bed every night? Or maybe G. K. Chesterton's Father Brown series? Or even C. H. Spurgeon's John Plowman series? What about J. R. R. Tolkein, or George McDonald, or Dorothy Sayers, or John Bunyan, or William Shakespeare, or John Milton, or Geoffry Chaucer? But don't stop with books. Fill your home with good music, beautiful art, challenging crafts, and lovely plants. Every one of us has limitations — differing gifts, skills, talents, and financial resources — but all of us can use what we do have creatively and wisely. Paperbacks, cassettes and posters are very inexpensive, and *anyone* can transform a pile of construction paper, glue, scissors, glitter, and crayons into a rollicking good time.

Conclusion

Dungeons and Dragons is a dangerous game. It serves as an introduction to evil, a catechism of occultism, a primer for the ABCs of the New Age. It is a recruiting tool of Satan. It can alter the daily behavior of regular players. It stimulates the seamier side of our imaginations. It is an enormously attractive and effective escape for people frustrated with life. For many it becomes pure, obsessive fantasy, in its most destructive form. It is no longer a game, an imaginative diversion, but a substitute universe in which the player pretends to be his own God and to make his own rules. *D&D* is not the only problem among young people. The statistics on teenage suicide, however misinterpreted in the major media, are indicative of widespread dissatisfaction and disillusionment among our youth. This is the larger problem that must be dealt with. And this problem is often exacerbated by *D&D*.

Games reflect, as well as reinforce, the faith-consensus of a culture. As such, *D&D* is the perfect game for the New Age '80s, providing the self-indulgent escapism of drugs without the harmful physical effects. You can get a kind of hallucinogenic high and still make it to the health club for your workout. Taking a wider view, we might say that FRPs take modernity to its logical conclusion. Since Descartes, modern man has retreated from the bright light of God's creation into the dark world of his own mind and imagination. Though his world is a dungeon populated by dragons, demons, and monsters, he says with Milton's Satan, "Better to rule in hell than to serve in heaven"!

Thankfully, as parents we can provide our children with wholesome alternatives. We can protect them from the strangely magnetic allure of the dungeon. We can win the war for their hearts and minds and souls.

If only we would.

FOR FURTHER READING

Al Ballard, *Answers to Common Questions About Dungeons and Dragons* (Los Angeles, CA: Christian Life Ministries, 1981), 9 pages.

G.K. Chesterton, *Orthodoxy* (San Francisco: Ignatius Press, 1913, 1986), 135 pages.

Mel Gabler ed., *Dungeons and Dragons: Educational Research Analyst Handbook* (Longview, Texas: Educational Research Analysts, 1986), 90 pages.

K.W. Jeter, *Dark Seeker* (New York, NY: Tor Books, 1987), 317 pages.

Will Niebling, *Educators' Use of the Dungeons and Dragons Game as a Valuable Teaching Tool* (Lake Geneva, WI.: TSR Hobbies, 1980), 3 pages.

What a Dungeons and Dragons Game Is . . . and What It Is Not (Lake Geneva, WI.: TSR Hobbies, 1980), 6 pages.

Gary North ed., *Journal of Christian Reconstruction, "Symposium on Satanism"*, Volume I, No. 2 (Vallecito, CA.: Chalcedon Foundation, 1974), 209 pages.

Unholy Spirits: Occultism and New Age Humanism (Ft. Worth, TX.: Dominion Press, 1986), 426 pages.

Walter Patinkin, *Introducing Children to the Occult* (New York, NY: Regis Lucifernus Press, 1979), 89 pages.

Phil Phillips, *Turmoil in the Toybox* (Lancaster, PA.: Starburst Publishers, 1986), 191 pages.

Lester Throcksel, *Up in Flames: The Incendiary Work in Modern Times* (New York, NY: Regis Lucifernus Press, 1977), 92 pages.

J.R.R. Tolkien, *The Monsters and The Critics and other Essays* (Boston: Houghton Mifflin Company, 1983), 240 pages.

Elizabeth Wilson, *Books Children Love* (Westchester, IL: Crossway Books, 1987), 330 pages.